CREATE A POWERFUL LIFE PLAN

3 Simple Steps to Your Ideal Life

Connie E. Sokol

Praise for *Create a Powerful Life Plan*

"In short: **Get the book**. Do the work. Live the life you have always wanted but have been too afraid to go out and get. Connie shares her bits of wisdom to make our lives that much easier. It's all there. All you have to do is believe.
~Lisa Swinton, Book Reviewer

"I just love Connie's books, they give me such a push to do what I know I can. This book empowers you to make small changes that will lead to an overall powerful life plan. Even if you don't like to write, just reading the book in a sitting, like I did, will clarify your outlook on life. I highly recommend this book. I'm buying copies for the women in my life."
~Christy Dorrity, Author, The 2012 Book Blogger's Cookbook

"As I followed Connie's book, I noticed I was a more attentive mother, spent more quality time with each of my children, and better controlled my eating. It was also easier for me manage my time and put first things first. I was able to have time to breathe and just be still. Connie is my kind of woman! If you are patient and put first things first, better things will come your way. Make it happen with this book!"
~Courtney Wilson, Book Reviewer

ISBN: 978-0-9890196-3-7

Published by Chawton Publishing 865 S. Oak Dr. Woodland Hills, UT 84653

Cover design by Kelli Ann Morgan
Cover © Connie E. Sokol
Typeset by Heather Justesen

Table of Contents

Dedication

To my fabulous family who daily make my Life Plan
meaningful,
and to all the brave souls who read this book
to embark on their own life adventure.

Acknowledgements

Thanking people who helped to make this book possible—this dream since elementary school—is a tall task, considering that the list goes as far back as my sixth grade teacher, Miss Hatch. It was Miss Hatch who took my Paul Revere poem to the principal (who asked if I really wrote it—it must have been *that* good), and who then told me that yes, it was *that* good.

It is not possible to list everyone who has shaped my life, and added a pinch here and a dash there to the concepts shared in this book. But at least I want to express my love, joy, and complete adoration for my family. Putting them first allowed the concepts in this book to smelt together under the refining fires of marriage and childrearing. Although helping women and families is one of my deepest passions, it would mean nothing to me if I couldn't come home to the ones I love. Teaching a wonderful two-hour evening class still does not compare to what I feel afterward, when I walk through the door of my home and hear "Mom's home!" In five minutes I'm in pajamas, ready for a fast game of Speed, and we're back to the norm. For me, that's as good as life gets.

I also express gratitude for Wendy Palmer Clegg, a trusted and patient friend who has supported me from day one; and for my sister, who during a family trip through Provo Canyon inspired me to action by commenting, "I can picture you up here, writing your book." My thanks to many friends who, knowing my dream and feeling my fear, have helped and prayed for my success. And my gratitude to the women I've been privileged to life coach, speak to, and connect with as they have created their own life changes. Their willingness to share of themselves—and some of their experiences in this book—has enriched my life and the lives of others.

Lastly, my sincerest appreciation to Emily Halverson for her excellent editing, Kelli Ann Morgan for her perfect cover, and Heather Justesen for her magical formatting skills. Without these women, this book would still be on the To Do list.

From my heart, I wish each and every one of you the best of love, happiness, and success as you embark on your personal life changes. Let me know how you are doing, what you are accomplishing, and how you are developing. My purpose in writing this book is the hope that it will help you and your family live a happier and more fulfilling life.

~ Connie Sokol

Preface

I get my best ideas vacuuming or cleaning bathtubs—I'm not sure why. In fact, most of this book came from doing those kinds of things that millions of mothers do on a daily basis.

On that note, mothers of all kinds (at-home mothers, partially at-home mothers, and can't-stand-to-be-at-home mothers) often feel that housework, and—let's be honest here—*childcare* are monotonous, unproductive, unappreciated, and not worth their time. Many at-home mothers would rather be *out there* doing lunch, or at least dressed to the nines once in a while.

On the other hand, some career moms have found that life *out there* is not as glamorous as they had hoped. They would love just once to be able to hang up the 9-to-5 briefcase, stop parenting from the phone, and take a hot bubble bath without a worry or demand.

No matter what their situation, too many women feel fed up, tired, restless, bored, frustrated, and emotionally empty. They are looking for what they can't put a finger on. They want a meaningful life, but they don't know how to find it. These feelings are real and if left unaddressed can lead to depression, hopelessness, anger, confusion, loss of direction, and just plain "wenchiness."

I am here to say it doesn't have to be that way. With a few changes, your perspective and daily life *can* be better. The keys are figuring out what you want, how to make it happen, and then keeping your life in balance as you work for those changes. That doesn't mean life would be suddenly peachy if you'd just get your act together, but it does mean that your ability to deal with and love life will vastly improve. Changing yourself is the only sure way to achieve happiness. If you're groaning right now, keep in mind the end result: you'll finally get what you want instead of repeatedly trying a different dance to the same old tune.

In this book, you will not be told what your life should be. Or be given a set of complicated instructions to remember each time you look in the mirror. Instead, you will be empowered to choose *your* ideal life and how to live it. You will make a plan and then baby-step your way toward it every day, week, and month, learning how to enjoy every single beautiful and sometimes surprising step along the way.

This joy comes not just from learning wonderful principles, but from practicing them. As your momentum builds with each step, you'll slowly feel a change within--slowly, because the day-to-day undercurrent of progress often goes unnoticed. But one day, BAM, you will also *see and feel* the change, and know that you'll never be the same again.

Prepare to paint a life masterpiece: *your life*. Let thoughts flow, dreams unfold, and your ideal life begin.

Introduction

If you are reading this chapter, CONGRATULATIONS! I usually skip the introduction, not realizing that the author mentioned some *really important* things that would have helped me understand that book I ended up tossing after the third page.

Here are some key tips to keep in mind as you embark on this journey of creating a Life Plan for your ideal life.

You must be ready. I mean *ripe*. I mean falling-off-the-vine-because-you-want-to-do-this-program-so-badly ripe. More than casually looking, you must feel you've finally found it, the thing you need/want/can't wait to begin. Only when you are sufficiently frothing at the mouth to change, then—and only then—can you begin the program.

So, you ask, *if I'm not frothing, should I go back to the couch and continue on in my threads-for-a-bathrobe, eating-chocolate-chips-from-the-bag kind of existence?* No. Go on to *step two* instead.

If you are not ready yet, just listen to my downloads or read the books, blog posts, or other resources at www.conniesokol.com. Do this for FUN. If you have forgotten what "for fun" feels like, start re-learning today. As you enjoy what you're learning, motivation will follow.

For example, suppose you're at your daughter's gymnastics lesson and you have a spare fifteen minutes. Should you pay bills, or read a fun book like *Life is Too Short for One Hair Color*? Go for the book, of course! Read not to improve your life, but simply to enjoy it.

When you are ready, really ready, read this book just *one chapter at a time*, even if it takes four years per section. Do not overwhelm yourself by completing the entire book in three nights (unless this is particularly appealing or you are snowed in). Cramming deep thinking and writing in a short time will create frustration and stress. DON'T DO IT! Write one page, read one chapter, and enjoy one section. This approach will be cheaper and better than therapy and—when combined with close friends doing the same program and high-quality cheesecake—the results will be astounding.

Actually do the suggested homework. Normally bookwork of any kind rates an excitement pulse equal to cleaning toilet scum, but I can assure you it's not that kind of bookwork. CAUTION: Do not do the homework exercises when you are trying to mend a Scout uniform or speed drive to baseball practice.

When else do you have time, you ask? Good question. The answer is that you have to *make* the time. That's right. Sit down with your family or significant other and discuss your goals. Say to your husband and/or children, "I need fifteen minutes to myself and so do you. You get to choose your thing as long as it does not involve money, blood, or illegal activity, and so do I. Isn't that nice? Then you get to briefly tell me later about your thing, and I get to go on at length and in great detail about mine." Sounds great already, doesn't it?

Here are some of the "fruits" of creating, and then beginning to live a Life Plan:

Greater happiness, with an improved quality of daily life
More self-discipline
More awareness of personal needs
More energy and more ability to find time for what's important
Less hyper-focusing on a significant other, co-worker, or children
Greater ability to love and not criticize
More hope and excitement about each day
Awareness of change, achievement, and success in weekly life
Improved self-esteem
Improved martial relationship
Renewed sense of self and life's purpose

The Back to Basics 8-week Challenge

Back to Basics is the name of my website where I share principles, practices, and posts on better balancing being a woman, wife, and mother. To help women put the principles I teach into their daily lives, I offer a twice-yearly online program called the "8-week Challenge." The principles in the online program include those taught in this book.

These are quotes from participants who used the principles in this book through the support online program.

"This has been a very good experience for me to envision and take strides toward becoming a clearer, happier woman."

"Feeling better about myself, and [my] personal progress and future through this program."

"I can't thank you enough for the incredible gift you have given me . . . . Thank you for your vision and making it happen."

"I am so grateful for this program. I don't think I could have gotten these things done if it hadn't been for the fact that I had to choose a goal and write it down . . . . Also, writing (taking time to write my own thoughts and feelings) has been so therapeutic. I'm actually craving the time to write again. It's becoming a reward equal to or better than food!"

So enjoy this journey. Creating a Life Plan is not supposed to be drudgery. It's your life! Have fun with it. Pick a special place (a park, a quiet room, a closet) where you go exclusively to bookwork your Life Plan. Put flowers in that area, buy a pretty pen or notebook, and bring your favorite decadent treat, one that makes you feel ultra-pampered. Use this time and program to reveal and develop the best, most lovely you, and enjoy the uncovering and remodeling process.

This is your life; create it!

Chapter 1

My Successful Life Change: From Housewife Slug to Happy Hot Mama!

What do you want?

This is the second scariest question a woman can face, only slightly better than, "How much do you weigh?" If you are like most people, this question will invite a blank stare and let-me-see-back-in-1985 stories. But knowing what you want is crucial. , Without that, you will never get what you want, be happy with what you have, or savor what comes your way.

Not knowing is a tough way to fly.

I had my own "What do I want" moment. Incidentally, and unbeknownst to me at the time, it's what would begin this whole life-changing thing.

What began my what-do-I-want journey was having four children in six years. At that point, my energy and most likely my brain cells were completely spent. At the start of the seventh year some energy returned—an inexplicable burst, in fact, during which I announced, "I LIVE!"—but it was more like the energy of a marathoner taking her last step before she's declared legally dead. Nevertheless, I was determined. My husband and I rang in the New Year waving our banner (okay, **my** banner), "The Year of Change." This had nothing to do with menopause and everything to do with finally setting goals and getting my life in balance. Pumped, juiced, smoothied, I made my plan, tacked it on the wall, and said with great gusto, "Big Mama is back!"

And then I forgot. Or maybe I should say that I slowly faded back into what I call "The Haze," where first you think about accomplishing your goals, then avoid thinking about your goals, and finally end with "What goals? I am woman, I am acceptable," and scarfing a king-size Kit Kat. Bottom line: I had zero life. Meanwhile between snacks I had hired a babysitter for a few hours each week to take the children while I went upstairs and did something somewhat enjoyable, although unproductive those rare times I could even remember what enjoyable was.

My epiphany came when on such a day I went upstairs, closed the door, and threw on the bed a remote control, a grocery list, a few books, and a goal list. I stared at them—totally devoid of emotion, and suddenly I wanted a Kit-Kat. Then uncharacteristically I turned on a daytime TV channel (since during kid "business hours" viewing was pretty much limited to *Blue's Clues*). A popular daytime talk show happened to be on, and women of all ages and experiences were sharing how they had been searching for answers about life and its challenges, where they fit in the universe, and much more.

Now for years I'd done some motivational speaking on the sidelines—a little at my university, a little at my church, a little more in the community. The speaking had developed into a sort of women's program, one that I had shelved every time I had a baby (note prior detail of four children in six years). Ironically, the program was to help women deal with life's challenges, find their place, and fulfill their potential.

So here I was watching this show with women asking questions I knew could be answered. I also knew the answers that could make them happy, and suddenly it hit me that I had something to offer. That was that. A surge of part frustration, part Big Mama welled within, and I defiantly turned off the TV, turned to the bookcase, and loudly shouted, "WHAT DO YOU WANT?" At that point I was, first of all, thankful for sturdy wall insulation, and second, fed up with my Twinkie life (looks good on the outside, no recognizable substance on the inside).

I ripped out a piece of paper and wrote in gashing letters across the top, "WHAT DO YOU WANT?" Not stopping to think about *proper* answers, I wrote furiously, straight from the gut: "Write a book, speak to women, sing, feel healthy" and more. Then, after only a slight pause, I turned over the paper and just as feverishly wrote, "What is stopping me?"

I watched my pencil confirm what my gut had been trying to tell me, but what I hadn't wanted to know: "Spending too much time on husband's business, lazy about my dreams, not making this a priority in my life," and on and on. Sitting back for a breath, I looked at my work. There squeezed onto only two pages of paper was probably the equivalent of three years of therapy. I felt clean, purged, and ready for action.

After sifting and arranging thoughts, praying and thinking, eating and pondering, I knew trying to achieve all of my goals at once would be overwhelming. My new mantra was to choose one thing and see it to completion. So I chose losing weight because, basically, I hated looking like a bloated turnip. Not wanting to become skinny-focused, however, I decided to first lose some habits: emotional eating, obsessing about weight, checking my thighs ten times a day, and other undisciplined behaviors.

This moment was big (no pun intended). For the first time in years I determined, truly determined, to have a healthy body and spend only the necessary time thinking about it. But more than that, I was focused on changing my whole life, and hoping to do it one step at a time.

I paid attention to people and ideas that reflected my goals. I cut out and posted on the wall a picture of a woman's body I knew mine could resemble without bizarre and drastic surgery. I got specific and realistic about exercise. Regularly hitting the gym was not an option because I had four little ones at home, but I found a body-changing program that I felt would work. After some negotiation, my husband and I bought free weights and took "before" pictures that made me cry. I made a plan, arranged babysitters, and—though I invited my husband to join me on this journey—didn't sit around and wait for the phone to ring.

I had my ups and downs. In the beginning, after four straight weeks of being "so good," I looked even fatter and wanted to cry. No, I wanted a really big cheesecake. But I hung in there and the very next week the weight started to come off like a fake sumo suit. Meanwhile, the kids got repeatedly sick, my husband's workload increased ridiculously, and I injured myself slightly (although with much complaint). Throughout the setbacks, I kept at it, seeing my goal to completion.

I noticed a startling domino effect. Because of what I was learning from my physical transformation—discipline, patience, and endurance, all just from controlling the chocolate intake—I quickly began to feel more self-control in other areas of my life. I had more energy and more clarity of thought. I felt more in tune with my feelings. I knew when I wanted and needed to write, to sing, to laugh out loud, or spend an overnighter with my husband. My thinking expanded as I freed myself from self-imposed limitations.

Once I heard a woman wish that she could stop the "global whining" of women who complained that they didn't have time to even go to the bathroom. The old me was this kind of whiner. The new me prioritized her time. Because my husband was self-employed and I was a partner, I had been heavily involved in the business. Recognizing that there were other things I wanted to do with my life and that he was qualified enough to do it solo, I cut down to bookkeeping and scheduling, then eventually bowed out completely. This created more "real time" to be alone with both the kids and with my husband. I felt free. I had choices again. I cut my longer hair to a short breezy style I had secretly admired and shamelessly added color highlights. Suddenly I felt girlish, feminine, and attractive.

These small changes led to arranging a babysitter for a few hours here and there so I could begin writing again, something I had craved since grade school but felt I couldn't justify.

Feeling more in control of my happiness and destiny, I was also calmer and more accepting of both myself and others. My husband's quirks and foibles didn't bother me the way they once had because my mind was zoom-lensed elsewhere. And because the frustration and dissatisfaction in my life was dissipating, there was more room for pure enjoyment. My interaction with my kids became playful; I was more patient and at peace. No more clock-watching or wondering if I should fold laundry instead.

My mindset had become Yoda-like: "Do or do not; there is no try." By September I showed my husband a wardrobe notebook filled with cut-and-paste pictures of my ideal outfits. I said to my sweet, "These are the clothes I want. How can we make this happen?" At first he seemed sort of surprised and said something like, "Great" (or was it, "Wait"?). I ordered the clothes in my December goal size and thought, *Hey, four months to work toward it; I can do this.* The clothes came in October. For fun I tried on the first, then the second, and then the whole wardrobe because now *I* was surprised: every single outfit fit. Each slipped on as it was supposed to and looked—even zipped up—just like it did in the picture. No bulges, no puckers, no camouflaging with a big sweater.

And so it was with my life. Not without bumps, bruises, and all-out trauma, mind you. But still, all the pieces started to finally fit. I felt happy, content, in control of what I could control, and "Oh well" about what I couldn't.

I returned to motivational speaking and a few years later, restarted an organization to help strengthen families. From these experiences and research, I created a program to help women change their lives. This book shares the Life Plan component to help you change your life, too.

Seeing my "Year of the Change" to completion wasn't just about finishing a goal. I had experienced a paradigm shift, a true life change. In the end, my biggest obstacle to overcome was not the numbers on my scale but my spirit. I needed to break free of self-imposed limitations—of what I thought I was and what I thought I could not be. Now my aspirations are open-ended. I'm still discovering new possibilities. Life is not just a list of should-dos and chores. My life has truly changed and become more than I hoped it would be. It only took me thirty-something years to figure it out.

Chapter 2

Create Your Life Plan:
A Personal Compass for Your Ideal Life

You've made it to Chapter Two; things are looking good already. Now I'll take you through the three simple steps of creating your very own Life Plan, which will serve as a blueprint for your ideal life. The Life Plan will help you discover your life purposes and desires, and then help you determine specific steps to achieve them.

A Life Plan gives you that starting point, pulling together the thoughts, dreams, desires, and want-to-dos from your head, and getting them down in an organized fashion on paper. This small but powerful principle works. Over the years with my Life Plan—and help from above—I've been able to write and publish books, be a national and local speaker, lose and keep off twenty-five pounds (seven pregnancies!), become more spiritually grounded, stay close to my children and teach them life skills, make and save money, travel, be a TV and radio host, and in general, create a more loving harmonious home (the latter is up for debate).

Why does a Life Plan work? Because it's a process of clarifying what you really, truly want from life, right now, and in the future. This clarity helps you decide how you'll spend your time, energy, and resources. And those choices will yield specific results.

David Allen, author of *The Art of Getting Things Done* says, "Thinking in a concentrated manner to define desired outcomes is something few people feel they have to do. But in truth, outcome mimics reality."

If you create a positive, inspired life plan, you will undoubtedly accomplish it, in some way, at some time, in your life. That's what's so amazing. Time and tide is on your side.

Before beginning, it's imperative that you do two things: first, sit up, take a deep breath, and say, "I give myself permission to be happy"; second, commit to **doing** what it takes to be happy, and trust that you'll know or find what that might be. Stop worrying that you do something bizarre, like move to Bali in search of happiness (though a visit, now that's a different story…) I firmly believe that all the ingredients we need for a happy life are within us, right now. Deep inside, we know what we need to do. We just have to get past our fears and defenses, and listen to that small voice that always speaks the truth. Think of that voice as the soft, creamy center in a chocolate-coated ice-cream cone. To start tapping that creamy center, let's get started.

The three simple steps to creating your Life Plan are as follows:

Create a Life Vision
Choose a Life Focus
Set ONE weekly goal to achieve it

Each step connects to the next, funneling the vision of your ideal life into doable, chewable chunks to be achieved over time. Even though the steps are simple, they are sometimes not easy. Each will require you to think, feel, and do. As you create the mental picture of your ideal life, you'll find yourself motivated and excited to start living it.

Chapter 3

Dream Big

Step 1: Create a Life Vision

A Life Vision is the first step in creating your Life Plan. Specifically, it's a paragraph comprised of four to six sentences that describe your ideal self and life—a written reminder of what you want your ideal life to be, feel, and look like. Then when you are faced with choices that are emotionally charged, your Life Vision acts as a neutral blueprint to restore clarity and remind you of your long-term focus. Though you will continually fine tune your Life Vision, your basic true needs and wants (healthy relationships, a purposeful life, etc.) will likely remain the same.

When describing what your ideal life will be, look, and feel like, it's vital that you be as specific and imaginative as you can. Research holds that if an emotion is intense enough and recurs often enough, our nervous systems experience something just as real, even if it hasn't yet happened.

That's a Life Vision. First, you clearly imagine the outcome, then using simple tools, work toward making that image a reality.

The Life Vision paragraph is broken down into three areas: Self, Relationships, and Life Skills. Choosing how you want to focus on each area is up to you. Self could include fitness, emotional wellness, hobbies, personal purpose, volunteering, travel, talents, etc. Relationships would include spouse, children, extended family, coworkers, friends, etc. Life Skills are those abilities that help you live a more productive and fulfilling life, such as good communication skills, financial savvy and budgeting, organizing your home, managing your time, etc.

You'll brainstorm words that reflect your ideal life in those three areas, then create sentences from those words. And lastly, you'll edit and compile them into one short, easy-to-remember paragraph that becomes your Life Vision.

Before You Begin

First, let's get the ideas flowing. Imagine that someone could grant your deepest wishes and give you your ideal life. Envision it. What would it look like, feel like, be like? What would you be doing, thinking, experiencing? What would you see, smell, taste, feel?

I have what I call a "Betty Crocker" version of my life. I am walking out of my beautiful home's French doors onto a sprawling wood deck. A perpetual size four, I am carrying a silver tray of delicious hors d'oeuvres that I just threw together. My husband waits with a cool drink for me on a shaded hammock swing where he will stroke my hair for six hours while we watch our teenagers play volleyball, after which they will eventually cook us a three-course meal as the sun sets. I am a happy, loving and loved, disciplined, knowing, and content woman, wife, and mother. And then I wake up. Sort of. I haven't yet achieved this *complete* vision (note, perpetual size four), but I am living most pieces of it *every single day*, right now. When you decide the outcome first, you make it into your own reality.

18

Now continue to ask more questions like the following to discover what you want:

If money were no object, what would I have/do/be that would make me happy?

If I could choose the people in my life, who would they be?

If I could be with the people I choose, what would my relationships look like?

If someone took care of the functional part of my life for a year, what hobbies/interests would I pursue?

If someone else saw me living my ideal life, how would they describe it?

If I could take classes in areas I am interested in or need to improve in, what would the class topics be?

If you're not sure what you want, listen to yourself. Get quiet and observe. I guarantee the information is already in your mind and your conversation. Listen to what you talk about. You'll notice a pattern, a continuous thread running through most of what you choose to discuss—topics such as money, weight, material objects, the faults of others, etc. You'll quickly see what subconsciously preoccupies you, both positively and negatively. What you find may surprise you. If you like the subjects that preoccupy you, write them down. If, on the other hand, you don't want to keep stressing about some things, prepare to list those preoccupations as things that won't bother you in your ideal world.

Write Your Life Vision

Below is a step-by-step explanation of the Life Vision worksheet, to be used in conjunction with the Sample Life Vision worksheet at the end of the chapter.

Brainstorm buzzwords that describe my ideal life:

In this section, write down your thoughts in single "buzzwords" that describe what you want. *No,* you say, *I hate to write!* Well, that is just too bad because your success greatly *depends* on whether or not you write this down. However, you can control how much you write down, so no need to make it a thesis.

If it helps, brainstorm words into three life categories: **self**, **relationships**, and **life skills**. Self could include words about your emotional, physical, and mental well-being. Relationships might have *clear communication skills, set appropriate boundaries, healthy connection,* etc. Life skills could include *financial, organization, running a home, time management,* etc.

Write your thoughts quickly and be as specific as you like. Write at least a paragraph and *don't self-edit,* just let it all hang out! Don't think about grammar or about whether your words make sense or are embarrassing or would make someone laugh. Just write or type the words you would use when talking to a completely trusted friend and great listener.

Take all the time you need. You may need a couple of hours, or you may work in spurts over a week. Some women have taken a few weeks to complete this step simply because it takes time to emotionally process such deep feelings. Often they have to open up, stop to assimilate and process new thoughts, then open up a little more, etc. Use a journal or binder to record answers, thoughts, and feelings and keep them all in one place.

Meanwhile, don't wait for the right words or until you have it "just so." Start. Put pen to paper, fingers to keypad, and just jot down thoughts like it outlines above. Put only the words that you *want* in your Life Vision, not the words you *think* should be there. You are not being graded and will not receive a gold star for the right buzzwords. Once you have it down, trust me, you will be ecstatic to see your desires in print, and it will look so doable!

CAVEAT: You may be tempted to skip this part and go see what's on the tube. DON'T DO IT. This is *your* life and it is passing you by. I did an exercise program once and the book said to write down what I did each day because there was nothing worse than losing weight and not knowing how you did it. "Well," said I, "once I'm in shape, I won't need to know how I got there, will I?" Guess what? I got pregnant and had to start all over. And where were my sheets? In a dusty book of half-words, half-hieroglyphics; I couldn't figure out a thing I had done. So write everything down— and legibly!

If you need more ideas about what you want, here are some buzzwords from other participants: peace, love, laughter, a safe haven, fun, relationships, wellness, celebration, close connections, calmness, invigorating activities, a true life partner, better self-knowledge, order at home, good health, sharing relationships, contentment, etc. People also mention actions like creating beauty, developing and sharing talents and abilities, becoming organized and disciplined, knowing how to relax, and feeling a sense of purpose.

Organize buzzwords into sentences:

Look at your buzzwords or categories. Now circle the most important or most repeated words (e.g. *peaceful, debt-free, organized*).

Write those key words into a sentence. For example, you might write, "Self: I see a happy, loving, spiritually grounded woman who contributes to her family and community."

Remember, this step helps focuses your vision. It's worth the effort, so stay with it!

Combine sentences into one paragraph that summarizes my ideal life:

Condense your sentences down to the most essential words that describe your ideal life. Lastly, create one small paragraph that includes one or two long sentences from each area (**self, relationships**, and **life skills**).

Condense final paragraph into one long yet concise sentence:

Be ruthless; take out any words that don't capture exactly what you're thinking. Create one long sentence or two for each life area (Self, Relationships, Life Skills) to be the foundation of your Life Vision.

TIP: Play with this! Type it, tweak it, cut it, and let it simmer. Think about what you have written and then pay attention to the answers. Eliminate what is confusing or doesn't ring true. Highlight words that come back to you. After this fine-tuning, put your paragraph somewhere you visit often. Above all, don't paralyze yourself with needing to have it right the first time. Think, write, cross it out, add more to it. Post it on a wall or your smart phone and let it develop.

One lady said it had taken her a long time to finally sit down and write it out. But when it was done, she said, "I just finished my life paragraph. I am soooo stoked! I am running around and shouting, wahooo! Thank you, I'm excited to see my life take shape from here!"

Here's a sample Life Vision sentence:

I am a loving, connected, growing, healthy, spiritually in tune, and grateful woman with connected, thriving, enriching marriage, family, and friend relationships based on love and agency, and I know how to prioritize, organize, and savor my life while making a positive contribution to the world.

One last thought. You can create your own Life Plan and do a stellar job. However, if you really want a true, solid, and tailor-made Life Plan that creates lasting change and develops all aspects of life that you deeply desire, I encourage you to involve Deity. Whatever your beliefs, take your Life Vision to God or that higher power and see what it becomes. I believe in God, so I take my particularly brilliant plans to Him through prayer. Time and again, He takes my seemingly marvelous plans, and reworks, enhances, or redirects me to make it better. Much better. Connecting with Him before, during, and after creating a Life Vision will truly change your life.

Congratulations—this is your Life Vision!

A Life Board

One woman who had successfully completed an exercise program shared that she used a wall of inspiration to keep her going. She would put pictures of athletes and other body shapes that mirrored her desire on the wall in front of where she exercised. I have expanded that concept, adding Life Goals and all things that motivate, inspire, and remind me to enjoy my life, and call it a Life Board. You can use any blank area on any wall, but if you're a perfectionist, feel free to get a whiteboard with nice die cuts and quill pens, and use meticulous calligraphy to write your goals. Just make sure you do it and make it work for you!

After completing your Life Vision, post it on your Life Board (hopefully somewhere easy to see). Depending on where you post it, every time you wake up, put on your makeup, or open the fridge, the statement will help you to subconsciously refocus on your Life Vision. Do not discount how much your brain can work on the issues, even while you are making breakfast, listening to a colleague, or sewing a parade costume. As Diane, an online program participant, said, "The [Life Board] is really powerful. Those little thoughts come from the subconscious . . . [to] help you get in touch with the real you!"

The Life Board *is* powerful! I've used them for almost ten years and can't even list all the amazing opportunities, experiences, character traits, and relationships that are part of my life because of posting it first. As you read magazines or hear relevant quotes, cut them out or jot them down. Make a collage of the goals you can't wait to achieve and personality traits you desire to develop. Believe in the picture you have created; it *can* be your reality.

Example: My Life Vision

To create your Life Vision, do the following:

Brainstorm buzzwords that describe my ideal life (relating to self, relationships, life skills, etc.):

Relaxed, more even in my emotions, connected without needing strict structure, balanced, focused, loving, in tune, healthy, happy, know God, savor each day, humble, generous.
Appropriate boundaries, good friends, not clinging, fun, involving my husband, children, just being, loving my kids, not hovering, delegating more, letting them choose, following through on consequences, more fun things together, prayerful

Organize buzzwords into sentences:

I am healthy, happy, organized, balanced, learning, confident, spiritually in tune, and at peace. I know my priorities and am willing to work and sacrifice for them. I show gratitude for life and love and share my time and talents in a meaningful way. I have a deepening, loving relationship with my husband—a relationship nurtured by mutual support, fun, peace, and involvement. We are independent but united and connected. My children are loving and loved, nurtured and serving, learning and connecting with their family and world. They know to love God and receive personal inspiration for their lives. My friendships are accepting, loving, and non-controlling. They ebb and flow, giving each person room to breathe. I know how to budget, cook, manage my time and space, and efficiently do the mundane tasks while finding the perks in the role I have chosen. I learn through each phase of my life what I need for that phase and then apply what I learn with love and gentleness to myself and others. I learn from mistakes, know when and how to relax, and stop negative thoughts

Combine sentences into one paragraph that summarizes my ideal life:

I am a loving, healthy, connected, balanced, growing, confident, and relaxed woman who is spiritually in tune, who sacrifices less important things in order to live by priorities, and who makes a difference in life. I am loving and loved. I have a connected, growing, thriving, enriching, and supportive marriage and friendships founded on love and agency. I know how to prioritize, organize, learn, apply what I have learned, savor daily life, and relax. I feel a spiritual connection to God, and I make a positive contribution to the world.

Condense paragraph into one long yet concise sentence:

My Life Vision:

I am a loving, connected, growing, healthy, spiritually in tune, and grateful woman with connected, thriving, enriching marriage, family, and friend relationships based on love and agency, and I know how to prioritize, organize, and savor my life while making a positive contribution in the world.

Connie E. Sokol

Template: My Life Vision

To create your Life Vision, do the following:

Brainstorm buzzwords that describe my ideal life (relating to Self, Relationships, Life Skills):

Organize buzzwords sorted into sentences:

Combine sentences into one paragraph to summarizes my ideal life:

Condense paragraph into one long yet sentence:

My Life Vision:

28

Chapter 4

Get Specific: Choose your Life Focus

A Life Vision gives you an overall picture of what you want from life. Now you can read the paragraph and say, "This is what I want and where I am headed." That said, what will you *do* about living your ideal life this year? This month? This week? What actions will you take in order to reach this year's end and say, "Wow, look how my life has changed and come closer to my Life Vision ideal!"

This brings us to the second step in this three-step process, which is to create a specific Life Focus. Without this, will look at that lofty paragraph, replete with passionate prose describing your ideal life, but still be left asking yourself, "How am I going to get there?"

To choose a Life Focus, thoughtfully read through your Life Vision paragraph. Choose one word or ideal in each life area of Self, Relationships, and Life Skills that resonates most with you.

Right now you might be saying, "But I want to change ALL the Life Areas!" You're not alone. However, you will be more successful, and happier, if you begin with one area, succeed at goal setting and achieving there, and then move to the next. If you're at a loss to know what Life Focus to choose, here are some ideas.

Do you want to change the physical you by getting fit, eating healthy food, or doing an all-over makeover?

In *The Confident You*, author Barbara Barrington Jones tells of a woman named the Ugliest Girl in Centerville, her hometown. This woman had been through many physical ailments and emotional struggles. At length this woman decided to focus on improving the physical and began an exercise regimen. She then went to a wardrobe consultant and discovered ideal colors and clothing combinations for her face and figure. Combined with on the efforts she made to improve her spiritual side (due to the domino effect), she changed her whole look. Today she looks like a Miss America!

Do you want to work on the personal you?

Perhaps you repeatedly do the same negative behaviors that you want to eliminate. In *Life Strategies*, author Dr. Phil McGraw states that when we do things we don't want to, and know it, we must be getting some kind of emotional payoff. For example, emotional overeating could be a physical buffer to keep people at a distance. Perhaps you could look for negative emotional payoffs in your life this year and focus on replacing them with positive payoffs.

Do you want to work on the financial part of your life?

Perhaps you want to start a business, but don't want to leave your small children. Consider this: the *Deseret News* reported that Julie Aigner-Clark, owner of Baby Einstein, was an at-home mother who started the baby instructional-video business by literally pulling props across a table in front of a Beta-cam. Baby Einstein grossed $11 million in 2000, and Aigner-Clark sold the business to Disney in November of 2002 for an undisclosed amount. All this was accomplished by a woman who quit her teaching job to be a stay-at-home mother for her daughter.

Choose your Life Focus

After reading through your Life Vision paragraph, and the above information, choose a Life Focus and write it down on the Sample Life Vision sheet.

For example, Jill's Life Vision included a variety of pursuits, but after reading through it, three particular areas rose to the surface as top priorities. These three areas became her Life Focus for the year: "I will strengthen my relationships, organize my home, and achieve physical well-being."

Choosing a Life Focus also jumpstarts the domino effect.

The Domino Effect

When you make one significant change, the new habit or attitude gained positively influences many areas of your life. This is called the domino effect. For example, after just a few weeks of creating and living a Life Plan, Laura wrote the following:

"I feel like this has had a snowball effect. I'm doing well in my focus areas, but I find myself doing more things that move me towards my goal even though I haven't written them down. For example, my focus this week has been exercise for me. I've also given up [soda], a daily habit not good for my body. I've started drinking water to replace it. And not eating sweets every day. It seems like I naturally do more than just what I've written down because the focus is more prevalent in my mind."

Another woman shared, "Now I'm seeing the domino effect we've been learning about. I have a new zest for life. I feel forward movement where before I felt I was just treading water and trying to keep my head out of water. I love my life!"

Focusing on only a few areas saves you energy, helps you concentrate, keeps distractions to a minimum, and helps you see excellent results quickly. Discipline helps you stay focused, and this focus then enables you not only to be more productive, but also to bring forth previously untapped ideas and understanding.

The domino effect works because change begets change. I can't tell you how many times I life-coached a woman who wanted to lose weight, and then began getting organized, or vice-versa. A goal to organize your closets often leads to changes like simplifying family routines, which then leads you to streamline your finances, and so forth.

Because of one focused umbrella goal, you ultimately achieve many goals in several areas.

Now it's your turn to choose a Life Focus!

[*For the following, refer to the sample Life Focus sheet at the end of the chapter*]

Life Focus for 2013:

Write a Life Focus sentence that includes three areas of your overall focus for this year.

Focus:

This year I am:

Self: _____

Relationships: _____

Life Skills_____

If it helps, consider beginning each focus sentence with the phrase "I see, I feel, I know how to" (see Sample Life Focus page). For example, for the Life Focus under Self to get fit and fabulous, you might write, "I see a vibrant, trim, and healthy woman. I feel energetic, positive, and confident in my body. I know how to eat healthy, rest regularly, workout appropriately, and listen to my body cues." As you create statements for each Life Focus area, what you need to do becomes more clear and specific. Use these brief thoughts to create weekly goals (i.e. eat healthy, rest regularly, workout appropriately). Fabulously simple.

Congratulations! You have created your Life Focus for this year. For convenience, transfer only your actual Life Focus to your Life Board.

As you specify and complete your Life Focus, you may feel like Tracy, a program participant who shared, "I feel like my life is moving forward . . . . Having the goals—a roadmap with a Life Vision and a Life Focus—makes all the difference!"

Example: My Life Focus

Life Focus for 2013:
> Self: *I will achieve physical well-being*
> Relationship: *I will strengthen my primary family relationships*
> Life Skills: *I will organize my life and home*

Self Focus: Achieve physical well-being

I see . . . *a healthy, balanced woman committed to a healthy lifestyle, good meals nicely presented, and healthy snacks.*

I feel . . . *joyful, relaxed, graceful, confident, energetic.*

I know how to . . . *relax or extend myself, to exercise in ways I enjoy, to live a beautiful life, to find appropriate energy, and to be wise and balanced in my activities.*

Relationship Focus: *Strengthen relationships*

I see . . . *a connected, loving, nurturing, growing, learning family, and friends who love to work and play.*

I feel . . . *content, peaceful, energized, accepted, happy, creative, and educated by all we experience.*

I know how to . . . *teach, listen, allow others agency, encourage, pray, support, love, and share.*

Life-Skills Focus: *Organize my life and home*

I see . . . *a clean, orderly, simply beautiful home that runs smoothly with routine but flexibility.*

I feel . . . *able to think clearly, at home, energized, at peace, in control of needful things, peaceful.*

I know how to . . . *file, manage time, budget, keep tax records for home/business, and teach these principles to my kids.*

Template: My Life Focus

Life Focus for 2013:
        Self: _____
        Relationships: _____
        Life Skills: _____

Self Focus:

I see . . .

I feel . . .

I know how to . . .

Relationship Focus:

I see . . .

I feel . . .

I know how to . . .

Life-Skills Focus:

I see . . .

I feel . . .

I know how to . . .

Chapter 5

Life Goals: Ready, Set, Goals!

You have now written an overall Life Vision and chosen a specific Life Focus in three life areas. You are fabulous! What do you do now? Whatever you do, do not fold laundry—in other words, do not get sidetracked. Do not let your excitement become only a past memory within two weeks. With a Life Vision and Life Focus, you have direction and intentions; now let's put those intentions into practice.

Select ONE Life Focus. Choose the one that really motivates you, the one you can't wait to begin!

Select a time period. Once you've chosen your first Life Focus, select a time period you want to complete it by. If you're doing a 4, 8, or 12-week duration, create one umbrella goal for that time period (i.e., Get Fit & Fabulous in eight weeks)

Choose ONE Life Goal each week that will allow you to achieve your chosen Life Focus.

Choosing a Life Focus and weekly Life Goals to achieve it creates simplicity, order, and concentration. These produce better results faster. It also eliminates inappropriate guilt. When the thought comes, "Gee, maybe I should organize my files," you can stop right there. Respond with, "No, that's not this month's focus; that's next month's goal," and you will feel peace, confidence, and control. Consequently, your goal-setting can lead to goal-succeeding.

Achieve ONE Life Goal a Week

For those of you who have ever meticulously written out New Year's resolutions, may I offer one wee bit of advice? Burn them. Research supports a conclusion I arrived at through personal experience years ago: Goals associated with New Year's resolutions will generally fail. This is mainly because the goals are generally not connected to a bigger picture. That's the purpose of your Life Plan—the bigger picture that connects and gives purpose to your individual goals.

With this program, I invite you to create ONE goal a week throughout your chosen time period. Weekly goals keep you stay consistently on track with your Life Focus. Someone once said, "The world stands aside to let anyone pass who knows where she is going." Weekly goals give you specific direction and better control over your pace. By concentrating your energy on one singular task, the achievement wheel begins to make substantial turns. After a short while you will see dramatic results because time and effort are not wasted in stops and starts. Creating weekly goals, followed by a weekly evaluation of that goal's effectiveness, guarantees the wheels of change will keep moving, (even if sometimes it feels like they're moving in six feet of mud).

Consider your Life Focus: In what ways can you accomplish that? What will you try? What appeals to you?

Brainstorm what might work best. For example, if your Life Focus is to "get fit and fabulous," then your weekly goals might include researching workout programs (weights, aerobic, stretching, etc.) or eating programs (low-carb versus low-calorie versus x-number of food groups, etc.), etc. This gets your mind thinking diversely and freely.

Using Your Weekly Goal Sheet

Next, choose your first goal and write it on the Weekly Goal sheet. I'll go through each section of this page so you will know how to complete it correctly. A completed sample of a Weekly Goal sheet is also provided at the end of this chapter.

How you write your goals is almost as important as what goals you write. The language of successful goals needs to be positive, precise, and in the present tense. Consider your goal a promise or a contract with yourself. As you *write* goals down, especially on a happily decorated Life Board, they become difficult to ignore. The goals also come to the forefront of your mind in a variety of situations throughout the day, tuning you in to opportunities you might not have otherwise recognized.

TIP: You may be tempted to write down more than one goal a week, thinking one goal is nothing, bupkis, nada. This inclination might be especially strong at the start, when energy and motivation are high and the chocolate withdrawals have not yet begun. But do yourself the biggest and best favor and STICK TO ONE GOAL A WEEK. Some of the most frequent comments from participants about what they've learned are to "simplify my expectations," "cut down my to-do list," and "reduce expectations to one—that quality is king!" Remember the domino effect and let things roll, but keep one focus in mind at a time above all others.

Rachel, a program participant, shared the following: "[What worked for me was] dividing my goals into tiny little chunks that open the door to a real life change. I am amazed at how close I am to achieving my goals by doing just little things, one week at a time!"

Example:

My goal this week: Have a 15-minute date with each child.

The following are some of other participants' goals:
Read three hours this week, nonfiction
Dinner preparation done by 4 p.m.
Establish a nighttime routine
Exercise four times this week
Give myself 45 minutes of alone time
Eat more healthy dinners
Make final plans for the yard
Pray every night
Connect with husband
Work on and complete my taxes

"How to":

After you write down your goal for the week, add a specific suggestion next to "How to." Include specific times, deadlines, numbers, and things to do.

Example:

How to: Spend fifteen minutes after dinner with one child while the other kids clean up; child chooses activity.

Participants share some examples of their how-tos:

Goal: Eat healthy for one meal a day / How to: Plan menus one week ahead

Goal: Exercise four times this week /How to: Get up at 5:30 a.m. and exercise until 6 a.m.

Goal: Read three hours this week, nonfiction /How to: After kids are down, read 30 minutes a night, six days a week.

Remember to make your weekly goals specific. One woman said, "Don't confuse good intentions with serious goal setting." Of course, good intentions are important, but statements like, "I'm going to get up earlier" or "I'm going to spend more time with the children" leave too much to chance. You haven't specified a method for reaching what you want. Successful goals mention specific to-dos and deadlines. Notice in the above participants' goals, they avoided vague statements, such as, "Exercise more often this week" or "Get up early to exercise."

In his book *The 10 Natural Laws of Successful Time and Life Management*, Hyrum Smith, CEO of Franklin Quest, shares five keys to making successful goals: *be realistic, timely, specific, measurable*, and *action-oriented*. Using these guidelines, your goals will be effective enough to propel you to success.

As you create weekly goals, don't stress about making them complex, but do read over them to be sure they give solid directions. The "Goal" addresses something you want to change;

the "How to" statement explains a specific, measurable, action-oriented way to achieve that goal this week. Below is a sample goal with various ways to complete it.

Example goal: Play more with the kids this week.
How to: Play games after dinner, go to the park in the afternoon.
OR Play fifteen minutes with each child, once each this week.
OR Park on Tuesday a.m., board games after dinner Wednesday for fifteen minutes, cuddle in a.m. before breakfast

The more specific your how-to options are *without boxing yourself in* (life happens; be flexible), the more likely you will be to achieve the goal. Using the above example (for instance), if it rains Tuesday, move the park excursion to Thursday and pull out the board games for fifteen minutes instead. Specific how-tos actually result in greater flexibility because you have created specific puzzle pieces that can be easily moved around during the week to best suit you and your family's needs.

On the other hand, try to avoid hyper-focusing on the specifics. It's more important to actually play with the kids in some form or fashion than to stick to the "How to" action you decided on last week—especially if it isn't making anyone happy. Feel free to add to or adjust the "How to" action in any way that makes accomplishing your goal more enjoyable.

Just for fun, here's a look at how the weekly goals might be achieved by this participant for four weeks.

Weekly Goals:

Have a fifteen-minute date with each child.
Date happened after dinner while other kids cleaned; the children chose the activity.
Take my honey to the mountains for a picnic.
Got sitter, cleaned picnic basket, bought goodies.
Read "Marriage is Like a Box of Chocolates" from Connie's workbook.
Read for ten minutes before bed.
Ask Julie for family birthdates.
Called Sunday, she e-mailed by Friday; wrote dates on family yearly calendar.

TIP: Create variety within your goals. Even though one Life Focus is to strengthen relationships, not every weekly goal has to include direct contact with people. In the examples above, notice the "dates" that directly involved people, but notice also that other goals included reading a book and organizing family information. Variety eliminates burnout!

Rewards:

Here, finally, is the really good part. You've worked hard all week, slaving over that goal, making those changes. Now it's time to choose your reward! By all means, choose something purposeful, enjoyable, and of course, affordable (personally, an uninterrupted nap is just about as close to bliss as it gets). Write your reward down at the beginning of the week so you are salivating by the sixth day. Who says life has to be drudge without a nudge? Or almond fudge?

Congratulations! You have completed the first half of the Weekly Goal sheet. Easy, easy, easy. Now just watch the changes happen.

Post your Weekly Goal sheet RIGHT NOW. Hopefully it will go on your Life Board, right under your Life Vision. It looks great. You're amazing.

Weekly Review:

Maybe just about now you are asking, "Hey, what's this Weekly Review thing?" Ah, the good news is, more writing! Even better news, it's all about *you*.

The Weekly Review is not a newspaper or a tax audit but a chance for you to reflect on the past week, on what worked and didn't work, and on what you will do differently next week.

At the end of the week, choose a lovely spot—preferably a *quiet* lovely spot. Take your favorite snack, pillow, pen, notepad, pajamas, earplugs, and escape to this lovely spot for at least fifteen minutes. (Do you see the pattern here, forcing you to take time out for yourself? Pretty soon you'll be begging for more writing forms.) This review is the time when you can determine, "Hey, this worked, this didn't, and, well, I drowned my sorrows in a hot-fudge sundae—what can I tell you?" The Weekly Goal sheet asks you five questions. Just answer them in order:

I wrote in my journal last week: Yes / No

Be honest. Circle yes if you actually put pen to paper, even if it was one sentence: "Was a complete slug." This helps you see the correlation between writing in a journal and goal success.

As one participant said, "At first I didn't like writing in my journal, I'm not a writer. But after a while I started to like it and found myself really looking forward to writing what was happening."

What worked for me this past week?

Summarize your experience for the month and jot down discovered behavior patterns or successful experiences. For next month's goals, you will know at a glance what personal principles to practice for guaranteed success. No matter what your method is, if it's working, fantastic. Wonderful. DON'T CHANGE IT. Remember, if it ain't broke, don't fix it!

Samples from of what worked: "My [Life Board]," "Recognizing things weren't all my fault so I could let go," "Checking in with myself frequently," "Saying no," "Asking myself before I eat, Do I want this? Is it helping me?" "Praying the night before," "Focusing on what was really important."

What didn't work for me this past week?

There it is in black and white: what didn't help you. Believe me, after you see this a few months in a row, it starts to affect you like teenager's laundry—you naturally want to get rid of it. Who wants to spend energy on doing something that isn't working?

Sample comments from participants about what didn't work: "Giving into old habits," "My goal wasn't specific enough," "Procrastinating filling out my report," "Having sweet snacks too available," "Feeling impatient with the timetable," "Need to set a consistent time for my goal."

What will I do differently next week?

Here you can evaluate what would actually help you next week instead of just repeating the "same old, same old" while expecting marvelous changes to occur.

Samples from participants of what to do differently: "Give myself credit for each step forward," "Hug and hold my children each morning [when] they awake," "Put my [Life Board] in view," "Keep positive by listening to positive music and reading positive things," "Work on my bedtime," "Write more in my journal to keep me focused," "Reach for healthier snacks first," "Take time to read instead of saying I'm too busy."

Comments:

Tell it like it is—what you thought, felt, experienced—the bottom line. Believe me, you will absolutely treasure these comments. They are a running commentary about you and your wonderful life!

Sample comments from participants:

"The days I read for fun I felt much more at ease and content. It was fun to have a storyline going on in my mind. I wasn't as intense with my family."

"I noticed a difference in my son's behavior and responsiveness toward me. Also, his morning greeting and excitement to see me and play. I love it!"

"I am really enjoying this! The real me got lost somewhere between the birth of my oldest child twelve years ago and now. My quest is to find her again this year."

Congratulations! Your Weekly Review is done! Put that sheet in your lovely binder or journal for reference when creating new goals in order to remember what has worked and what hasn't.

A weekly review is absolute gold! It helps you understand, appreciate, and adjust your plan. Enjoy it. Look forward to this weekly alone time. And remember, this also means you have just completed an entire week, one step closer to your ideal life. This is a good time to reward yourself.

If you are brave of heart, I also recommend doing a monthly and yearly review. I do one on my birthday—pulling out my Life Board, putting stickers on what I did fabulously (yes, stickers), and making notes for what to improve for next year.

Go somewhere beautiful and enjoyable, even schedule a rejuvenating overnighter. Jot down thoughts or feelings in your journal. I promise that reviewing the year will bring a particular feeling of gratitude to both you and your children, not just for the goals you achieved but for the time you were able to spend writing about the experience.

Wow, you're done. You have just completed your Life Plan!

Hard to believe that at the start of this book you might have been thinking, *A plan? A vision? A focus? WRITING??* And yet here you are, completed and successful.

Continue to play with this Life Plan; think about it and allow it to germinate. Although I encourage you to keep the same Life Vision for the entire year so you can see real change, feel free to adjust, change, or all-out scrap something if you need to and start new weekly goals.

This is your life! When you get quiet and listen to the thoughts and feelings that come to mind, you will find the best rhythm for your goal-setting and life living. When in doubt, go with your gut.

Example: Weekly Goal sheet

Starting/Ending Date: *January 5-12*

My goal this week:
Read "Marriage is Like a Box of Chocolates" from Connie's workbook.

How to:
Before bed, read for ten minutes, six days a week. Keep workbook by bed, get kids down on time.

At the end of this week, I can't wait to reward myself by:
An uninterrupted bubble bath

Example: Weekly Review

I wrote in my journal last week: <u>*Yes*</u> / *No*

What worked for me last week?
Reading some of the book right before bedtime. Sharing what I read with my husband. We had a good talk and laughed!

What didn't work for me last week?
Trying to read during basketball practice. Not explaining to the kids what my goal was.

What will I do differently next week?
Tell my children my reading schedule so that they will have quiet time at the same time so I can read! Encouraging my husband to have some time to himself to read or do something enjoyable.

Comments/experiences:
Found myself looking forward to my nightly reading ritual and enjoying it instead of cramming it in between errands.

Template: Weekly Goal

Starting/Ending Date:

My goal this week:

How to:

At the end of this week, I can't wait to reward myself by:

Template: Weekly Review

I wrote in my journal last week: *Yes / No*

What worked for me last week?

What didn't work for me last week?

What will I do differently next week?

Comments/experiences:

Chapter 6

Challenges, Obstacles, Difficulties, Oh My!
Tips for Overcoming the Tough Spots

It's a fact of life: as soon as you create a goal, you can expect opposition. As you set goals, ask yourself, *What is likely to stop me? What will some of my challenges likely be?*

In *Awaken the Giant Within*, Anthony Robbins shares some history from the life of Michael Landon, a beloved man, actor, and director who suffered many obstacles in his youth. Landon grew up in an abusive home, was a chronic bed wetter, and had a mother who frequently staged suicide attempts and beat him. By the time he reached high school, he was skinny, experienced uncontrollable facial tics, and was filled with fear. Landon says what changed his life was the first time he even threw the javelin, throwing it thirty feet farther than anyone else. He says on that day he discovered something he could achieve and grabbed hold of it.

Grab your goal. Hold on for dear life as the waves rock you. No matter what comes, hold to what you know is the right goal for you, and with time, diligence, and prayer, you will most assuredly achieve it.

As you prepare to face obstacles, here are some negative feelings to guard against, as well as some suggestions for handling them.

It's just not a good time right now.

You're not ready, you say. Life is busy. Too many people and things need you. You need more time to prepare, know what you're doing, or have your life be in better order.

Suggestion: Do ONE thing to help you accomplish your goal.

Just do one thing this week, even if it seems difficult, or even insurmountable. Break your goal down into chewable chunks, and just do it. Say you have a goal to advertise your home-based business. Instead of mentally taking on that goal at one time, break it down to chewable chunks: make one phone call a day, talk to a friend in the same field, or meet with a community business-planning mentor (free services are available in many communities). Ignore the mental voices filling you with doubt. Take that math class. Paint that painting. Sit at the computer and write one chapter, even if it's drivel.

Years ago I had a goal to write this book, originally titled *Are You Ready for a Life Change?* In a terrific burst, I wrote a rough draft, which then collected dust on the shelf for far too long. I finally reminded myself this book had excellent principles and needed to get out there. Ironically, within a week of making the goal to finish the book, I "happened" to meet two women who liked to write and were willing to form a writing group at the same time. This is how goal-setting ultimately works. You make a decision, and then little miracles follow.

Don't wait for the perfect moment or situation; likely you wouldn't notice it or be prepared if it actually came. It's through *the process* of working toward your goals that you become ready for and create those perfect moments. In *Women of Influence*, authors Pat and

Ruth Williams share how Oprah Winfrey experienced doubts about her new opportunity as a talk-show host in Chicago. Winfrey would be the first black host of a show in a racially hostile city. Winfrey had told her manager the reality: she was black and overweight, both of which were not likely to change. Her manager simply said to be herself, and the rest is history.

I'm afraid.

Fear is a serious demon. Every one of my books, CDs, and downloads was almost naught because of fear (okay, and several children). Giving into fear stops our progression and hinders our positive contribution to others.

Suggestion: Set a deadline.

If you find yourself afraid to start, there is nothing better than forcing yourself to begin by a serious deadline. In fact, the reason this book is in your hands is because I scheduled a blog tour for the book. Suddenly, the concept became reality, and I had to put my backside in the writing chair and get it done. On time. Regardless of sleep deprivation, the busy lives of seven children, or my goal to lose five more pounds. Ironically, I was able to do all of the aforementioned, mainly because of the adrenaline surge that accompanies said deadlines.

In addition to setting deadlines (and *especially* in conjunction with them), invite the power of prayer. In my life, prayer has been the greatest factor in overcoming my deep-seated fears. Before speaking to an audience of 600, writing my first book, and filming my first TV show, the fear I have felt has been almost unbearable.

But prayer has brought me peace, direction, and perspective that has helped me hold my ground and be my bold self.

I don't have enough time, money, or energy.

One participant said her whole perspective changed at one of our retreats when a life coach had her list what she wanted in life and then added, "Now eliminate the question of time, money, or ability, because those can be overcome."

Suggestion: Find your purpose.

A few years ago I had the goal to write *Faithful, Fit & Fabulous,* a core eight-week program helping women to set and achieve eight goals in eight weeks in eight life areas, such as get fit and fabulous, balance womanhood and motherhood, etc. But with several children and busy schedules, I debated about whether I had the time or ability to do it. However, as I focused on the *purpose*—sharing solid principles that helped women and families be happier—I became creative with my time and energy. I typed the manuscript at ballet and art lessons, and while my youngest went to kindergarten. Not only did I finish the book, but went on to write and publish several more. That's the power of a Life Plan.

You may feel you have purpose but don't have the resources. Years ago when I originally decided to print the gift book *Life is Too Short for One Hair Color*, I didn't have the extra $2,000 I needed. A short time after I made that goal, however, my husband happened to install a hardwood floor for a man who owned a printing establishment. Supporting my dream, my husband did the work as a trade in a win-win situation for both the client and me. The point here is not that my husband is an amazing stud-muff-extraordinaire (this is a given). The point is that the resolution came *after* the setting of a goal, despite the originally bleak circumstances. First, *you* must decide what you want and the personal purpose behind it. Then life can help you move forward.

Another benefit to finding your purpose is that once you do have resources, you're motivated to use them wisely. Mary Kay Ash, founder of Mary Kay and a master of time management once said that those who are successful know how to effectively use their 1,440 minutes in each day. She noted that people usually give themselves a set amount of time to get ready in the morning, but if they wake up late can still be ready much faster. People who reach their goals learn to be efficient on a regular basis, rather than just in times of crisis.

I don't believe I am supposed to or really can have what I want.

Suggestion: Re-program your mental tape.

Surround yourself with positive statements. Read motivational books, ponder to know your purpose, and learn from others who are successful, both spiritually and temporally. Attend quality seminars, talk with positive people about how they get what they want, and make notes for yourself. Write your Life Vision and post it in a well-trafficked spot.

I don't want to take time from my family.

Suggestion: Level extreme thinking.

Not many people I personally know feel more strongly than I do about placing family above business. But our thinking—especially women's thinking—about this topic can become too extreme, and that's when we start to feel suppressed and consequently depressed. Create your vision and share it with your family. Discuss with your husband or a good friend how to break your goal into chewable chunks according to your season of life.

Family comes first, no doubt about it. But placing family first does not preclude doing anything else. It does mean involving them, influencing them with your dreams and goals, and overcoming struggles in ways that will benefit all of you.

I had six pregnancies in ten years and with my left toe did a program for women, then called LIFEChange. At times I would become frustrated with the stops and starts, never being able to jump right in and do it the way I wanted. However, I kept my promise to put my family first, and through that perceived sacrifice, my original program developed into an even better one. Every time we do the right thing for the right reason *first*, we will receive benefits we could not imagine.

During my busy times, I put my work with women and families on the back burner, doing just a little speaking here and there. Yet I involved my family in every way possible, and it became a bonding experience. We have delivered newsletters around neighborhoods on the four wheeler (all five of us on ONE four wheeler), vacationed together in various states in conjunction with my speaking assignments, and laughed at our family funnies in my printed columns. This is a family deal, and that's what makes it fulfilling.

Your life is yours. There are many things you can do right now to fulfill your dreams, but these things won't become clear until you stop hyper-focusing on the obstacles. Challenges and obstacles will always be a part of every person's life, thank goodness. Through overcoming them, we become stronger, wiser, and able to give back more to those who will encounter them in the future.

As you become aware of your particular challenges, use these tips and others you discover to continue building strength and ability throughout your life-changing experience. When you bring about positive change, fulfill a dream, or develop a good new habit, you feel energized and refreshed; life is good and savory. Suddenly, no matter what the day brings, you don't wake with a cringe and a headache, already anticipating the worst. You wake ready to live your ideal life!

Chapter 7

The Good, the Bad, and the Ugly:
What Do I Do When I'm Stuck?

You've written them, sung them, and tap danced them, but still your goals are a series of stops and starts. You're frustrated, raising your hands to the heavens and crying, "WHERE'S THE JUSTICE?" Or the brownies, I might add.

If you hit a stretch of confusion, lack of motivation, deep frustration, or just plain blahs, you're not alone. Read the following statements and questions that we often hear from our participants. Maybe our suggested solutions and answers will help.

I'm confused. I don't understand what I am supposed to be doing.

Relax. You're normal. Many people who create a Life Plan for the first time feel the same way. Go back to the beginning of the book and start with a small section. Start with something that interests you. If you're confused about the forms, e-mail us at www.conniesokol.com. Tackle them one form, one day at a time. Do not overload your circuits with too much new information. Try one step and let it settle. Then try another, and so on. Changing your life is a long-term process, not a race.

I really don't know what I want or what I'm trying to achieve.

Fundamental questions like "What do I want from life?" are some of the toughest we can answer. Remember, the first part of this life-changing process is really about getting your bearings. Experiment with different goals; try out new ones as if you were shopping for what kind of Life Vision pleases you. Give yourself some breathing room and your true desires and focus will eventually surface. I promise. Keep choosing a weekly goal that appeals to you, and ask yourself which of the goals you've tried has deeply motivated you. In the long-term scheme of things, a few weeks or months is not such a long time for discovering what you really want. You likely have many, many years of a higher quality of life ahead of you!

I've lost my motivation! What do I do now?

The comments we read most frequently from participants during their first few weeks suggest that people generally try too hard at first and then get discouraged, but eventually find their rhythm.

BIG QUESTION: Are your goals *should dos* rather than *want to dos*? Sometimes we set goals based on the approval of others or to fulfill someone else's expectations. Generally, doing something we aren't truly committed to results in zero motivation. If you lack the get-up-and-go, change your goals to an entirely different area (example: changing your focus to Life Skills or Relationships, etc.)

Only write down those goals that you are completely and totally excited about, and DO NOT ALLOW YOURSELF TO FEEL GUILTY. Using positive goals as motivation is entirely necessary to catapult the domino effect into action. Have faith that you will do the *shoulds*, but remind yourself that right now you get to focus on what you *want*. Focus on one goal that brings you true joy and you will find the energy and motivation to do ten *shoulds* without making them into goals!

Am I achieving something? Is it working?

Great question. We planner-minded people can be used to grades, stickers, or at least to-do lists with tasks we can cross off to show we are progressing. Ask yourself at the end of the week, "Have I grown? Did I do/experience/consider something to do with my Life Focus?" If you did, you're succeeding.

If you still need a ranking system, I invite women to rate their goal achievement between 1-10 at the end of the week. An 8-10 is success! Remember, we're aiming for a working 80 percent *before* we try for a flawless 100 percent.

If you felt you didn't achieve what you should have, consider the following possibilities: goals were set unrealistically high; goals were vague and without deadlines or specific how-tos; goal setting was chaotic, hit and miss, hard to understand, etc.; more than one goal was written, making you feel overwhelmed. Remember that achieving our goals through baby steps allows us time to healthily assimilate change. It's very important that you start with goals that are small, but still make you stretch (e.g. exercise two to three times a week if you haven't been regularly exercising). Then get them down to an automatic rhythm and enjoy them. This is much better than making extreme goals (e.g. exercise four times a week) and having to berate yourself for not reaching them.

Finally, remember that some progress, like losing weight, is not immediately noticeable. You can't always see the progress until, one day, your pants just fit better.

I've been doing the program, but I feel stagnant. What can I do?

Try one of the following suggestions:

Change one variable. If you exercise in the morning but it's blah, do it in the evening, wear or buy a different outfit, change your mode of exercise, etc. Shake things up a little.

Years ago, I wanted to write a book and made the goal to type in our alcove early every morning. I never did. A friend arranged for me to come up to a mountain cabin for a few days to write, and I completed the entire draft in three days. Sometimes if you change one thing—environment, time, components—you'll find your motivation again.

Do your Life Board. Post fun quotes or pictures from a magazine, book, or inspiring movie. Use a key word or photo to remind you of a specific goal. I taped a picture of the Statue of Liberty to represent my goal to visit New York (for both writing and pleasure), and presto—I fulfilled my goal.

Talk to someone else who is creating a Life Plan. You can connect with them at www.conniesokol.com. Share but don't compare. Post insights, progress, struggles, and triumphs necessary for any success. Enjoy getting input and congratulations from others.

What if I want to keep the same goals from week to week or month to month?

Here is what Sheri, a program participant, shared:

"Last month I knew what goals I needed to set and work on. I knew what BIG changes I needed to make. But this week I couldn't come up with goals that felt right. I have a whole list of things I eventually want to do and change but none of them felt good. That's when I realized I needed one more month to focus on things I've been doing so they become true habits and part of my daily life no matter what. So I'm keeping the same goals but worried about staying motivated, so I've added a focus project that goes with that goal."

Feel free to keep the same goals, but as this participant recommended, add some different angles or spice to them so that they don't become boring.

Can I keep one goal but add another one during the same week?

I have experienced this myself. I am exercising and want to remind myself to keep that up, but it's not my main focus. Remember, not everything has to be a goal. Put a Post-it note on your Wall of Inspiration to remind yourself of your "maintenance" goal, the one you already are doing well. Then use the new goal as your springboard for the next week.

What if I have tried to do the program, but my heart isn't in it right now?

Put it aside. Remember back at the beginning when I said you must be ripe? You must want change more than you want an all-expenses-paid week in Tuscany. You must be screaming for it.

"But," you say, "I thought I *was* ripe." Well, you weren't. Not ripe enough. If you don't feel into it, *do not* think you have wasted your time because you have *absolutely not* done so.

I believe in a "primed point." These are points we sort of "pressure cook into," points that require time, experiences, and even testing underneath the lid before we are ready to all-out explode with purpose. You have probably been testing under the lid, peeking, and putting it back down, saying, "It's not ready yet." When you feel that primed point, go with it. I believe that each time we look under the lid, we look longer and harder at what we have to face, and gain confidence in our ability to do so.

To get to a more primed point, listen to motivational podcasts, read blog posts, or watch video segments on the eight life areas at www.conniesokol.com. After doing some of these, I'm guessing your motivation will get a boot in the bum.

Chapter 8

The Secret to a Successful Life Plan

When we moved into our new home, I noticed my neighbor had planted two long rows of pink peonies. They extended out from her front door to the sidewalk, and they were full, bushy, and exploding with color. These flowers brought to memory an experience I had had the year before, just a mile down the road in our previous house.

Wanting to be *Green-Thumb Wife Extraordinaire*, I decided to plant pretty spring flowers in my yard. The closest I had ever been to yard work had been as a teenager, weeding our yard for $1 per garbage bag. When the helpful man at the nursery I visited asked if I needed soil, I—Green-Thumb Extraordinaire—thought, *Hello, the soil is already on the ground!* Politely, I declined, thinking, *Soil? Get some new help around here, people.*

Excited to prove my gardening prowess, I began digging holes for the 30 plus plants I had bought at the nursery. After spending about half an hour to dig one tiny hole, finding cement-like clay and many, many, many rocks, I noticed a small problem: I needed soil. And that wasn't all. To make these plants grow, I needed about twenty-five other things (a pick, a garden fork, a better shovel, gloves, a stronger back, fertilizer, and a teenager to do all the work). And quite frankly, it was close to lunchtime and I was losing juice. In typical form, I dug shallower and faster, threw all the plants haphazardly into the ground, and said, "Well, I'm sure they'll be fine."

Three of my plants survived.

Now, getting back to the Effortlessly Successful Gardener Neighbor. Her flowers were blooming outrageously and yet I rarely saw her out there tending them. I kept thinking, *How did she get her flowers so big, so quickly, so easily?* One day while chatting, our conversation just happened to specifically hit right on that question. "Oh," she said, "I just use Miracle-Gro."

And that was that.

What does this have to do with your stellar Life Plan? It's basically this: you can do this program and you can do it on your own and see some wonderful results. Or you can use some spiritual Miracle-Gro and see results that you would never have on your own.

Some of you may think, *Whoa Nellie, back the horse up a minute. Did she say the word "spiritual"?* Before you leap to visions of brown robes and monotone (albeit, very beautiful) singing, know that your spiritual side is real—even if you don't wear a brown robe. If you want to see change—dramatic change that is specific and right for you—you must discover and involve a spiritual dimension in your life.

Let me make something perfectly clear at the outset of our spirituality chat: I am not suggesting we just throw a bunch of emotional plants in the ground, pour on the Miracle-Gro, and then go to sleep. Obviously my neighbor had put time and energy into proper planting and maintenance *and* used the Miracle-Gro.

To tap into your spiritual side, starting simple may be best. I am no spiritual giant, but I can suggest two basic places to start: ponder and pray. No matter what your specific spiritual beliefs are, pondering and praying are two of the surest ways to clean out your mind and clarify your perspective. Neither of them is mystical or mysterious. Prayer is very simply asking for help and being grateful for blessings.

Although I know many people whom I consider to be more spiritually centered than I am, I do know the benefit of prayer. Having had four children in six years, I could share more than a few experiences. (I could also share a few experiences about the benefit of self-medicating with Cadbury's chocolate and creative uses of duct tape. Perhaps another time.) Anyone who says she has never prayed doesn't understand the nature of prayer. Many of us pray all the time. When we get the tax notice, the overdue mortgage statement, the wayward child, the challenging coworker, we pray. Usually we say something very basic like "HELP ME" or "What in the world am I going to do now?" or "I can't handle this!" or "How will I make it through this ordeal?" Prayer becomes more effective, however, when we consciously acknowledge that some higher power might actually be listening. Saying, "Dear God, please HELP ME," or "Dear God, please help me get through this ordeal" makes all the difference.

Though there are also other things we can say, and in a manner more befitting when speaking to Deity, the point is the communication line is opening. Give it a try. You will feel lighter, happier, calmer, and partnered in your life, especially as you move forward with your Life Plan. If at the very least you begin to see God as a good friend, you're tapping into the spiritual Miracle-Gro.

Now let's discuss pondering. Pondering is like meditating, which Webster's defines as: "To think deeply and quietly [. . .] To consider at length: contemplate." (Strangely, though, the dictionary doesn't say "To ignore small children banging on the bedroom door: to completely disregard wailing.") Pondering or meditation is simply being still, taking time to allow the matters of your soul to settle and sift into sense. I'm sure you've already done this at some point in your life. The key is to get off the fast track long enough to meditate on a regular basis. I try to practice ten minutes a day of being still (note the word "try"). Believe me, if in a day I accomplish ten minutes of stillness, everything else on the schedule is a bonus.

I've noticed this also works with my kids. Out of necessity, I began having them rest for ten minutes in the afternoon (simply because if they are not resting, I am not resting). The rule is, they have to lie still. This, basically, is torture for a seven-year-old. But it works. We actually enjoy ten minutes of sheer quiet, a feat more amazing than world peace, and its benefits carry over into the next several hours.

Stillness has also helped me to realize how quickly I am moving from thing to thing (I call this "pinball living") instead of giving myself time to assimilate what is happening, how I feel about it, and what is essential to me. I get all this from ten minutes of daily meditation. (If it could also reduce the size of my thighs, it could be a program all by itself.)

Another way to ponder is to read something inspirational. Don't read for speed; read to feel what you believe and know to be true. As you do, you will feel strengthened. Like not knowing you were thirsty until you drank water, you will come away feeling rejuvenated and fulfilled in a way you didn't know you needed.

So this is my "spiritual Miracle-Gro" thought for the day. I do know that prayer and pondering works; it's kept me sane through the adventures of life, marriage, and motherhood. Hopefully you too will find a method that helps you tap into this spiritual connection and support and then watch your peonies bloom!

Chapter 9

The Amazing but True Effects of a Life Plan on Spouses, Families, and Friends

Yes, a Life Plan will do wonders for you personally. But just as the domino effect influences change in every facet of your life, so it will with your family and friends.

Spouses

When I taught classes for women at a conference facility, a male videographer who taped my presentations took me aside after a class on "Balancing Womanhood and Motherhood," and said, "Connie, this experience has influenced my marriage!" He shared that the comments and principles helped him to better understand his wife and her needs. For perhaps the first time in twenty-five-plus years of marriage, he went home and asked his wife to take a night out for herself. He supported her efforts to pursue her interests, and this ultimately changed their relationship!

Later, this man's son happened to produce my first audio recording of "Balancing Womanhood and Motherhood." Again, I discussed the principle of a weekly night or time out for each spouse. The father relayed to me weeks later that while taping my talk, his son had listened closely and later suggested to *his* wife that she should take a night out for herself. The father shared that his daughter-in-law had always been a wonderful woman, but that now she had a new spark and vivaciousness about her.

Just hearing about your Life Plan, and your experiences in developing it, can help loved ones not only better you, but desire to improve their own quality of life. A short time after one of our women retreats, one participant went home and shared the concepts she learned with her husband. It prompted her to ask him what *he* wanted from life, what his dreams were, and what direction he wanted to go. What followed was an insightful, connecting conversation where they made key turning-point decisions for their future. As she later said to me, "This really works!" A spouse is especially, but not exclusively, affected when participants' goals specifically involve them.

Another participant, Brianne, shared the following:

"I started an 'I love you' journal for my husband for Father's Day. Every day I wrote a paragraph or two about what he did that day that I appreciated, or just nice things about him. It is amazing that when you are REALLY looking for the good (not just saying you are!) it seems like your beloved can do no wrong. We make our husbands into who we think they are. Don't you just love these mini-revelations as you go through life? I am so excited!"

My sweet husband, who loves me more than his DeWalt saw, has practiced many Life Plan principles in our marriage. In fact, he has gotten to the point where he can often feel comfortable reminding me, "You know, honey, I'm not feeling very validated here." This can be annoying. On the other hand, how wonderful it is to share this kind of understanding and communication together. As another woman said, "My husband is starting to talk [like the program]."

These life-changing can principles apply to everyone: men, women, youth, senior citizens, married, and single. However, it is my experience that Life Plan principles are most influential and effective when started by women. As they learn, so do their families.

Jeanette made a long-term goal to "Reconnect with the things I love" and then a narrower goal to start mountain biking again. However, because she had neglected this hobby as she had raised her kids and worked part-time, she also had to make goals to get the bike back into commission, purchase a bike trailer, and reserve time once a week to ride her bike. This is what she wrote about her experience:

"The presentation (on pursuing passions) was awesome. I really remembered that I loved biking so much. I started thinking, my life is not going to be put on hold because I have little children. Although my youngest can't ride in the bike trailer until she's eighteen months, I'm still going to take the older two boys (one on his bike) and ride. My husband will love spending the time with the youngest. [One Saturday] he took us up to the bike trail and we had a ball. My son said, 'This is the best bike ride of my life.' It made me feel SOOO happy. I totally need to do more with him [besides telling him] 'clean up your room,' 'brush your teeth,' 'stop playing Nintendo.'"

Jeanette's goal was to reclaim a passion, but in the process she also spent more quality time with her family and strengthened her relationships with them.

For another woman, what started as a goal to strengthen relationships with her children turned into an invitation for closer ties with extended family. Keri decided to plan weekly summer field trips for the children. Together they made a list of all the activities they wanted to do and then planned the summer schedule accordingly. As the plan evolved, she decided to invite her family members to do the same with her. This is what she wrote:

"This was great! I made a great list of field trips, wrote my sister a great letter expressing a desire to build a relationship with my kids, their kids, and them. I shared my desire to support each other as mothers and how I felt that this summer we could have fun, get close, and uplift each other through our challenges. I am so excited about this goal—I really think it will strengthen all relationships involved—mother-child, sister-sister, aunt-nieces, and nephews, cousins!"

Here was a woman whose goal to strengthen relationships with her children dominoed into involving her extended family.

Lori, who had a large family and had not taken time for self-enjoyment, shared the following:

"Last week I went to dinner with a friend and then we shopped for four hours! It was so fun! I came home way happy. A couple [of] days later I was wearing a blue sweater I had got and my eight-year-old son noticed and asked if that was what I bought the other night. Realization—our children needed to see that we love ourselves enough to serve ourselves, too."

As you live your Life Plan, share with a trusted friend or family member what you're experiencing. Your new thoughts and actions will likely inspire them to feel more empowered to achieve their own goals.

Friends

One program participant made a goal to expand her home-based tutoring business. Through this goal she eventually created tutoring kits to be used by other mothers who wanted to tutor children in their home. At one point, her friend's husband lost his job, and the family was in financial difficulty. This participant got her friend started in tutoring, and within a few weeks the friend had a full tutoring schedule and was making great money, which helped their family in a time of crisis and encouraged them to continue in their own life changes!

Applying basic, true principles will have a domino effect in your life and the lives of those around you. Personal relationships are fundamental in our lives, and when we affect them for good, we make positive change. Anytime we set and achieve goals that directly or indirectly relate to what is most fundamental in our lives, we increase not only our own happiness but the happiness of those around us.

As you read in the next chapter about specific experiences of five women who have created and developed a Life Plan, you'll quickly see that although they are all very different, most of their goals revolve around important relationships. Even their skills-related goals such as organization and time management end up enhancing or improving their personal relationships.

Chapter 10

A Life Plan in Action!
The Experiences of Five Women

To give you a better idea of a Life Plan in action, here are five women's experiences. I've included each woman's Life Vision and Life Focus, as well as three to five sample goal sheets from her online program. I've again changed all names and distinguishing characteristics so that they have no reason to egg my house.

Julie

Life Vision: I envision myself at peace in a fun environment with close connections with family and friends.

Life Focus: I will organize/prioritize my personal schedule so I can enjoy my time and relationships.

Weekly Goal: Tracking my time

How to: Keep record of what I do/ how long it takes

Reward: A trip to [my favorite ice cream place] for ice cream

Wrote Journal: Yes

What worked: Keeping track (on paper) of what I do and how long it takes

What didn't: Trying to fit an unrealistic amount of activities into my day

Do differently: Simplify my expectations

Comments: I realized and accepted that getting my preschoolers ready and keeping them happy takes a lot of time. For the first time I decided to accept and enjoy that rather than change/deny/rush it. I think this will help with the "at peace" part of my Life Vision.

Weekly Goal: Make a livable schedule

How to: Write down/focus on a few necessities, leave time to have fun

Reward: Ice cream

Wrote Journal: Yes

What worked: Not trying/wanting a daily house cleanup

What didn't: Trying the afternoon schedule I set up—too rigid

Do differently: Loosen up in the afternoon—plan one thing for the morning and one thing for the afternoon only

Comments: Taking time to think and plan my future and present life gives me more self-awareness and value. It's depressing to see how little I can actually put on a daily "to do" list aside from/in addition to the survival skills for our family of eight people.

Weekly Goal: Giving my kids complete attention when we're talking.

How to: Stop whatever else I'm doing, eye contact, really listen

Reward: Going somewhere fun on the weekend

Wrote Journal: Yes

What worked: Conscientiously stopping and making eye contact pulled me into the child's conversation and I really enjoyed interacting with them rather than half listening and not really hearing what they're saying.

What didn't: Not doing it often enough

Do differently: Try to combine this (with my next goal) EVERY TIME they say something

Comments: Thanks for doing this program!

Weekly Goal: Having a fun outing with each child

How to: Son—birthday party, sports sign-up
　　　　　　　Three oldest girls—Olympic activity nights

Two youngest—individual playtime

Reward: Having a Jacuzzi with music and candlelight

Wrote Journal: Yes—my weekly psychoanalysis of myself

What worked: Relaxing, doing something fun for our relationships; taking a break from a serious-oriented goal

What didn't: Procrastinating filling out this report

Do differently: Go back to a serious goal again—staying positive during cleanup and homework with oldest children

Comments: It was good to enjoy the Olympics with my children. I wouldn't have wanted to miss that because I was concentrating on an unrelated goal. It worked for me to look at what's going on in my life and tailor the goals I have to the events during specific days or weeks.

Anna

Life Vision: I want to be in love with life. I see myself sitting on the deck, holding my husband's hand, watching the kids play tennis, enjoying the mountains and beautiful landscape of our yard and vegetable garden.

Life Focus: Strengthen relationships with God, myself, husband, friends, and family

Weekly Goal: Reading for enjoyment.

How to: Read one chapter Tuesday, Thursday, and Saturday

Reward: I'm going to get my massage this week!

Wrote Journal: [not marked]

What worked: This week's goals were wonderful! Being all by myself, alone, in a quiet place reading was the best goal ever!

What didn't: This pillar is really weak and needs a lot of strengthening. Everything really fell into place this week! Yeah!

Do differently: [not marked]

Comments: The [Life Board] is really powerful!

Weekly Goal: Getting the kids ready for school.

How to: Being awake and home between 7 and 8 a.m.

Reward: Getting another massage!

Wrote Journal: No

What worked: My goal was to give my husband more free time from 7-8 a.m.

What didn't: Stressing out over not getting enough sleep causes me to lie awake until 3 or 4 a.m. By Friday I had the worst headache I've ever had in my life.

Connie E. Sokol

Do differently: Try to accommodate my husband yet not let my good habits slip.

Comments: This was my hardest and most discouraging week so far! This must mean real progress, huh?

Weekly Goal: Finding something positive in something my husband does and telling him one thing daily!

How to: Making a small chart and marking it with a sticker or tally mark each day I'm successful

Reward: Getting a massage

Wrote Journal: No

What worked: [not marked]

What didn't: [not marked]

Do differently: My relationship pillar with my husband is one of my weakest pillars. This week and month I am going to quit dancing around it and hit it hard on the head!

Comments: Last month in class we discussed pursuing our passions! I knew I would have to rediscover whatever my passions are (It's been a long time). The next morning a friend called and asked me to take a sign language class with her. I'm going to take the class to see if it rekindles a passion.

Emma

Life Vision: I want a warm welcoming home, built on a foundation of Christ filled with love, peace, harmony, joy, laughter. . . . A safe haven where family and friends and our children are drawn to. I want to enjoy fulfilling, loving, supporting, connected, peaceful relationships with my husband and children. Also to have a few lifelong, meaningful, real connected friendships.

Life Focus: I will prioritize my time so I can strengthen the four most important relationships in my life.

Weekly Goal: Having special time with each child

How to: Spend a minimum of fifteen minutes playtime with each child

Reward: Pedicure, facial, tanning pass, and new perfume!

Wrote Journal: Yes

What worked: Being more focused on playtime. I just played whenever he said, "Play with me, Mom" instead of saying I've got to do this or that.

What didn't: Having a set "special time" after getting dressed, etc.
Do differently: In order to do it I had to put him off until I was ready. Instead I found it worked best to play with him as soon as he woke up in the morning, so that's what I will continue.

Comments: I noticed a difference in my son's behavior and responsiveness toward me. Also, his morning greeting and excitement to see me play. I love it!

Weekly Goal: Exercising daily and following a low-carb, low--fat diet

How to: Going to bed at 10:30 p.m., getting up before kids at 6 a.m., motivation project and wall of inspiration poster finished

Reward: Painting my room and buying new curtains for it!

Wrote Journal: Yes

What worked: I did great for four or five days, followed my plan diligently

What didn't: I'm finding that my pattern is four or five great days, two or three off days when I get discouraged. Then I start over, recommit for four or five great days, two or three off days. It's leaving me with an unsuccessful feeling. I wasn't even motivated to do my wall of inspiration since it was in my two or three [off] days that I'd planned to do it.

Do differently: I have to keep reminding myself of the overall positive effect and changes I've made instead of the daily successes I haven't made.

Weekly Goal: Begin and commit to a weekly family night

How to: Make a family chart, write and work on a family mission statement, talk with my husband about time commitment, make a plan, do it!

Reward: Going somewhere fun on the weekend

Wrote Journal: Yes

What worked: I picked up a mission statement packet, working on it, made my chart, and held family night. Also worked on a plan for future family nights.

What didn't: Making my goals too late in the week when my husband was out of town to do it.

Do differently: To have our family night on Sunday night when he is always home.

Comments: We'll give it a try.

Weekly Goal: Increasing my patience and love, controlling my temper when handling the kids

How to: Pray, be consciously focused on doing things with love, take time out, breathe, count to twenty or longer if needed

Reward: [not marked]

Wrote Journal: No

What worked: Being focused on handling things/situations with love and kindness. I'm sure praying for patience helped but really focusing on changing the way I was emotionally reacting. I found myself filled with more patience and I handled little "explosive" situations without reacting with a temper. I found my son doing things more willingly and independently.

What didn't: Nothing.

Do differently: I will continue working on this but I am being even more sensitive to the way my emotions/reactions affect my whole family atmosphere

Weekly Goal: Practicing effective communication with my husband and showing my love for him.

How to: Study daily the effective listening/expressing steps, use them; daily express appreciation and give sincere compliments; greet him with hug and kiss, positive attitude

Reward: Buying a new scrapbook binder

Wrote Journal: Yes

What worked: I felt more positive and had a better attitude—expressed my love, spent time with my husband and felt very loved and appreciated back

What didn't: Sick kids, lost my focus. I don't feel like I got many chances to use effective communication or maybe I don't understand the steps well. I didn't feel like I used/studied it enough.

Do differently: I need to make some goals that are not so "heavy"

emotional, physically, etc. They seem to be weighing on me daily.

Comments: I need next month to try some "one time" goals instead of "every day do this" kinds of goals

Nicole

Life Vision: I embrace life as an amazing gift from God to be enjoyed and celebrated every day. I joyfully share my talents and abilities.

Life Focus: I am daily discovering, nurturing, and rejoicing in who I really am and the difference I can make.

Weekly Goal: Replace three negative thoughts

How to: Repeat three replacement faith statements ten times, three times a day, and as needed

Reward: By Friday enjoy a healthy treat I don't usually get

Wrote Journal: Yes

What worked: Attending [a program presentation], using my thought replacements

What didn't: Feeling sorry for myself

Do differently: Accept the illness I've been experiencing and how hard it's been
Comments: [not marked]

Weekly Goal: Developing a new talent

How to: Practice the organ twice a week

Reward: Read for an hour a book of my choice

Wrote Journal: Yes

What worked: Following through on my goals

What didn't: Criticizing myself

Do differently: Be gentle with myself

Comments: I have felt a wonderful camaraderie [sharing with other women], like we're going through similar struggles and searching for similar answers, like I'm not the only one. Setting weekly goals and being accountable has been a struggle at times, and yet an exhilaration, a quiet sense of satisfaction. I feel like I'm going somewhere, like I'm charting a course of progress. It has given me a sense of focus, little stepping stones to mark my travels, a structure I have craved. Thank you.

Weekly Goal: Not eating after 8 p.m.

How to: Unless necessary or a special occasion

Reward: Going to a musical with my daughter
Wrote Journal: Yes

What worked: Sticking with the same goal. It's especially challenging for me because my husband enjoys his nightly ritual of late ice cream (my favorite!) and chocolate chip cookies! Enjoying time away with my husband and receiving some impressions in response to prayer

What didn't: The comparison trap! A constant, ongoing retraining process for me—years of habit to replace

Do differently: Focus on hope for the future, not fear and the difficulties of the past

Comments: Thanks for your comments in class about not comparing and being limited by *should.* I need that reinforcement so much!

Tasha

Life Vision: I want to be free from nagging worry by being well in body (mind, health, finances) and spirit (with God and family).

Life Focus: I will organize my home, work with my husband to pay off debt and begin to pay off home more aggressively; enjoy my husband and children through allowing them to learn and make mistakes—let go!

Weekly Goal: Organizing
How to: Throwing out clutter

Reward: Buying a book I want

Wrote Journal: Yes

What worked: Staying home more, only going out when necessary. Having more time to think. Throwing out junk!

What didn't: Doing too much in each day, sleeping in

Do differently: Pick one new task (main) each day instead of 2-3. Plan out each day.

Comments: That was great to get rid of that junk! It helped me feel more organized. This has been so much fun! I'm loving my life more. Thank you for this opportunity.

Weekly Goal: Writing

How to: Write to family and friends—yearly newsletter; this has been a goal of mine for years

Reward: Taking some time out on Tuesday night by myself—go to the library or read by myself

Wrote Journal: Yes

What worked: Wrote newsletter and had husband run copies—this helped! Talked to my husband about my need for more time out. He agreed to support me in this and gave up his basketball time on Friday so that he wouldn't be gone so much. I need to talk to him more—not wait until I get desperate!

What didn't: Made too complicated of meals. Must simplify! So there's more time to relax with the family after dinner

Do differently: I need to simplify my life by making simpler meals. I spend too much time in the kitchen!

Comments: I am finding that I want to focus more on essentials. I tend to get bogged down with extra nice to-do things and that leaves little time for relaxing with family or myself. Gotta get rid of extras!

Weekly Goal: Sleeping

How to: Going to bed by 10:15 pm

Reward: Staying up late! Just kidding! Calling my sister in Wisconsin

Wrote Journal: No

What worked: Seemed like nothing

What didn't: This was a very hard week. I felt very out of sync. The hardest part of feeling this was seeing how to get [out] of the hole.

Do differently: Well, I think watching the Olympics too much contributed to my funk. I'm not usually a TV watcher so this was off form. It's hard to be balanced with this lifestyle. I'm not going to watch TV this next week (little to none).
Comments: [not marked]

Weekly Goal: Getting better organized

Connie E. Sokol

How to: Getting files in order

Reward: Spending an evening at the library by myself

Wrote Journal: No

What worked: I finally organized my files—this has been on my "to do" list forever. I like to go up in the office and just look at them! Isn't that funny?

What didn't: I slept in too much

Do differently: Get up early and exercise. This really charges me for the day. I feel excited to dive into the day when I do this.

Comments: I realized at our last [program] meeting that I really need to work on my wall of inspiration. I haven't dreamed of what I want so this has limited me so much. This is a good idea—the wall!

Weekly Goal: Involving my family

How to: Cleaning out the basement during spring break

Reward: Going to a [program] meeting on Tuesday night

Wrote Journal: Yes

What worked: This has been therapeutic to clean out and get rid of "old garbage" in both ways—with my whole family! It felt good!

What didn't: Stayed up late and slept in late—spring break

Do differently: Back on my exercise early program that I've missed and been trying to get back on

Comments: It seems to work for me to set one goal to accomplish each week instead of one that involves every day involvement—for now, that is! It's more manageable for me.

Miscellaneous comments from other goal sheets:

"I think I was making my goals too hard the last couple of months. I made simple goals this month and things I really wanted to do. It was fun to do and accomplish these goals instead of a chore!"

"I've been using spare bits of time to read . . . it has all served to help me work toward wellness. I'm beginning to see how very hard I am on myself and on my family. I really want to overcome this habit."

"I like having one goal per week because it's easier for me to keep focused (or to do it)."
"After three months I'm feeling more focused on my Life Vision and Life Focus. This has been an added catalyst for change for me!"

"This last week was packed with lots of commitments but I prepared at the beginning of the rest of the week. So what would have been a very difficult week ended up being a really good week. I feel like I stretched myself and learned so much about my capacity! I can do more than I thought before!"

As you see from their shared experiences, these women are just like you and me. They have good weeks and tough weeks, but they are creating constants in their goal-setting, achieving, and recording. As they see weaknesses, patterns that aren't working, or frustrations that can be eliminated, they make a new plan and give it a go. All the while they are adjusting their day-to-day lives to better reflect their ideal lives.

Chapter 11

Change Your Life with Your Laptop: Doing the 8-week Challenge

You're ready. You've created a Life Plan: a Life Vision of your ideal life, a Life Focus for this year, and specific Weekly Goals to achieve the Life Focus. Wow. Great job. Buy some earrings. You are prepared for change. Now what?

Doing an 8-week Challenge

Making a change, any change, and especially a *life* change, can be tough, but everything that you have read in this book will help you succeed. I know because I did my own life change, a wonderful experience, and I did it basically alone.

Basically. But not completely. Because no man, or woman, is an island. Your chances of success will be much greater if you will follow the suggestions below and lean on the support provided within the materials mentioned.

Use this book to create a Life Plan, definitely. Then, if you feel you need a bigger boost, more information, or surefire accountability, join one of our 8-week Challenges. Through a challenge, you can tidy up your life to a working 80 percent by achieving eight goals in eight weeks in eight life areas. It's a great way to learn how to set and achieve a goal, while accomplishing some of those annoying, taunt-you-from-the-corner goals (i.e. organize your files, clean out the "craft/spare/scary room").

In a nutshell, this online program helps you apply the chapter principles in real life to see real change.

Using the Faithful, Fit & Fabulous book, each week you read a chapter, set and achieve one goal in that chapter topic (life area), and reward your efforts. You also receive specific resources, such as motivational video segments, podcasts, blog posts, and articles on the chapter topics. These resources help you learn how to set better goals, as well as stay motivated to finish them. Your efforts also enter you in drawings for prizes and downloads.

We officially offer the 8-week Challenge twice a year (January and September). However, you can receive similar life coach help through the *"Faithful, Fit & Fabulous:* The 8-week Challenge Podcast: Week by Week Life Coaching." This 60-minute podcast guides you week by week, step by step, so that you get the life-changing help you desire.

After completing an eight-week session, we encourage you to do another one that now solely emphasizes one of your Life Focus, such as Get Fit & Fabulous. Again, you'll receive specific motivational information to help you achieve your life goals. Find out more at www.conniesokol.com.

Highly Important Components for a Successful Life Plan

To absolutely ensure we have given you all the success information you'll need, here are a few tips for making this program successful in your life.

94

Read through the book thoroughly. When it says to write something down, write it down. I know: bossy, bossy, bossy.

Check out our website at www.conniesokol.com for tips, ideas, motivation, and inspiration. E-mail any questions that arise.

Use the right program products. I know, I know. You're thinking, *Aha, finally, the shameless plug.* No. I personally don't take any compensation for what I do with my Back to Basics program. But I mention the products for a reason: they work. Here's just one example: A woman purchased the "Balancing Womanhood and Motherhood" CD; she told another lady how great it was, who then bought the CD and loved it so much she lent it to her sister, who then refused to give it up, after which the original sister came back and bought another one. And so it goes. This is why I originally wrote the books and sat in a studio—very pregnant and uncomfortable—and recorded the presentations: because they *work,* and to get them into every woman's hands who could benefit by them.

Let your loved ones in on what you are doing so that they don't get a big shock. They cannot be supportive about something they don't understand. You will be making changes, and sometimes change is scary. Suddenly Mom is getting a life. Apparently a sister is losing weight and doesn't want fried chicken at the reunion. Move forward by selectively sharing (to whom and how much is up to you) what you're doing. When you feel the need, ask for support and help from the people you trust the most.

Speaking of friends, grab one, grab two, grab a gaggle. Go to dinner once a month or have a girl's night to share the principles you're learning. The more support you have, the more likely you are to succeed. If available, attend a live presentation to get extra motivated (check availability at www.conniesokol.com).

If you don't choose to create and live a Life Plan with friends, at the very least get one friend to whom you are accountable. THIS IS SO IMPORTANT. Over and over we hear from the women that accountability keeps them on track. In choosing a friend, as the movie says, "Choose wisely." You know the friend that always listens to you, commiserates over Rocky Road with you, and says, "Oh, I know, yes, that is *so* sad"? Not her. Do not, DO NOT choose her. Get the other friend, the brash, brazen but good woman with a good heart who will honestly tell you what you look like in a swimsuit should you ask. *That's* the one you want. A little healthy fear will keep those weekly goal sheets coming.

Visit www.conniesokol.com and my social media to find out what other women are doing to create and live their Life Vision, Life Focus, and Weekly Goals. Ask questions, read comments, offer suggestions, and share experiences.

Do the small things! Reward yourself, make your Life Board, write in your journal, post your goal sheets right where you can see them. Every bit helps—tremendously, unbelievably—so enjoy doing the things that matter most.

Chapter 12

Commonly Asked Questions about Back to Basics

What is Back to Basics?
Back to Basics is a website to help women get back to what matters most in life. I share principles, practices, and posts on how to better balance being a woman, wife, and mother, and enjoy it more fully. We use the book, *Faithful, Fit & Fabulous*, as a weekly guide during our 8-week Challenges. This book teaches simple principles and practices to better manage your life.

How do I begin an 8-week Challenge?
Everything you need is provided in the *Faithful, Fit & Fabulous* book. The format is sleek and simple: set and achieve one goal a week, for eight weeks, in eight life areas that need a boost.

Each week you will choose one of the eight topics (see below), read the chapter, set a goal, and then achieve it for one week. Finally, you can clean out that closet, organize those files, or create a cheery craft room. You choose the life area, you choose the goal, you receive the reward for the work (my favorite is free time to read or write!)

Choose from the eight areas as you desire: Holy Habits, Create a Personal Plan, Joy in Womanhood, Feel Fit and Fabulous, Balance in Motherhood, Get Organized, Develop Healthy Connections, and Establish Financial Peace and Prosperity.

Do the challenge with us twice a year, or do it with our online podcast "coaching" that walks you through the 8-week program, week by week. Continue to do the program for as many or few weeks as you like, stopping to take a break when vacations or craziness hits. No clubs to join or online accounts to maintain. Simply use the book and begin—or grab a friend, sister, or mother and do it together! Feel free to share your experiences at www.8basics.com. Enjoy!

Where can I get more ideas for using Back to Basics principles?

Check out the Back to Basics website for fun support and ideas. Check out "B2B Tips" on topics such as Fit and Fabulous, Get Organized!, etc. You'll find "Connie's Columns," my previous self-development columns written for the *Deseret News*, and weekly personal blog posts, as well as helpful products and participant experiences. If you can't find what you need, feel free to e-mail me at www.conniesokol.com.

Where can I find your products or schedule Connie for a speaking assignment?

Go to www.conniesokol.com and click on "Products." You'll find downloads, MP3s, podcasts, and more on each of the eight life areas. To schedule a presentation, click on "About Connie" or "Media." If you can't find something you need, feel free to e-mail me using "Contact Us."

My Life Vision

To create your Life Vision, do the following:

Buzzwords that describe my ideal life (relating to self, relationships, life skills, etc.):

Buzzwords sorted into sentences:

Sentences narrowed into one paragraph to summarize my ideal life:

The paragraph condensed into one long sentence:

My Life Vision:

My Life Focus

Life Focus for 2013:

Focus:

I see . . .

I feel . . .

I know how to . . .

Focus:

I see . . .

I feel . . .

I know how to . . .

Focus:

I see . . .

I feel . . .

I know how to . . .

Weekly Goal Sheet

Starting/Ending Date:

My goal this week:

How to:

At the end of this week, I can't wait to reward myself by:

Weekly Review:

I wrote in my journal last week: yes / no

What worked for me last week?

What didn't work for me last week?

What will I do differently next week?

Comments/experiences:

About the Author

Connie E. Sokol is the mother of seven, a national and local presenter, and author of several books including *Life is Too Short for One Hair Color Series, Faithful, Fit & Fabulous, Motherhood Matters,* and award-nominated romance novel, *Caribbean Crossroads.* She is a contributor for KSL TV's number one morning show, "Studio 5," and a regular blogger for KSL's "Motherhood Matters." She is the former radio host of "Ask a Woman." With her left toe, she delights in being with her family, taking naps and eating decadent treats. To schedule Connie or for more information on products, podcasts, social media, 8-week Challenges and more, visit www.conniesokol.com.

Made in the USA
Lexington, KY
23 November 2015